A KING STREET BOOK

Jesus the helper

by Christine Wright

illustrated by Eira Reeves

Scripture Union Publishing London
Sydney Cape Town Philadelphia Toronto

Acknowledgements

Author: Christine Wright

Illustrations: Eira Reeves

Cover design: Tony Cantale Graphics

© Scripture Union 1990

Published in the UK by Scripture Union, 130 City Road, London EC1V 2NJ
Published in Australia by Anzea Publishers, PO Box 115, Flemington Markets, NSW2129
Distributed in South Africa by SUPA, 83 Camp Ground Road, Rondebosh 7700
Published in USA by Scripture Union, 7000 Ludlow Street, Upper Darby, PA 19082
Published in Canada by Scripture Union, 1885 Clements Road, Unit 226, Pickering,
Ontario L1W 3VA

ISBN 0 86201 694 0 UK   Jesus the helper
ISBN 0 85892 459 5 Australia

Printed by Ebenezer Baylis and Son Limited,
The Trinity Press, Worcester and London.

Dear Parents,

Welcome to King Street!

We hope that this King Street book, 'Jesus the helper', will help you and your child share time together with God.

Along with the King Street residents, your child will discover basic Bible truths and stories which will help her discover how special she is to God.

If spending time with God is a new venture for you and your child, here are some ideas which will help you as you use King Street together.

• Try to find a regular time when your child can be sure that she has your undivided attention. Perhaps this could be during the day, rather than at bedtime.

• Focus on the value of the time you spend together, not its length. Five minutes may well be long enough some days.

• Have a Good News Version of the Bible close at hand to look up the references or to show your child where the story comes from.

• If there is an introductory story strip before a series of readings, read this to your child first. It will help to establish the story in her mind before it is serialised in the readings.

• Have a pencil and some crayons ready to use. It would also be useful if you read ahead to see if any extra materials are need for the next day.

• The 'Prayer time' every day will give you prayers and ideas. Use these as a springboard for your prayer time together. Encourage your child to suggest prayer items and to pray out loud.

Some days a box like this will appear:

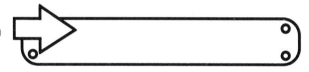

This contains extra ideas about developing the themes touched on in that day's reading. Do not feel you have to use them all!

It is a privilege to be able to help children listen to God as he speaks through the Bible and to help them grow in a relationship with him that is right for every stage of their development.

We at Scripture Union hope that the King Street series will help you in this. By looking at both the Bible and every day life, we hope that the times you share together with God will be very special.

Mary Hawes
King Street Editor

Contents

Meet the Miller family. They live in King Street. Mr Miller is a postman.
Mrs Miller works in the King Street opticians. Mr and Mrs Miller have three
children. Ben is five, Amy is four and David (who is adopted) is also four.
They have a dog called Robbie. Look out for them as we go down King
Street.

A paralysed man

The children at King Street playgroup, were playing a game called 'Hop Stop'. While Mrs Graham played the music, they all had to hop around the room. When the music stopped, they all had to stop too.

It was great fun! Some of the children wobbled a bit while they were hoping. They had to use their arms to help them balance.

Jesus met a man who couldn't use his body at all. Matthew 9:1-8 tells us how Jesus helped him.

The people who saw Jesus help the man were amazed! Join the dots to see what they said.

Praise God

Can you hop? Which parts of your body do you need to use?

Lord Jesus, you're great! Thank you for helping the man who couldn't move. Please help me to be a good helper too. Amen.

Two blind men

'Close your eyes,' said Mrs Graham one day at the King Street playgroup, 'and we'll play a listening game.'

David closed his eyes and waited.

'What am I holding?' asked Mrs Graham. There was a loud banging noise. 'It's a drum!' shouted David. 'Well done,' said Mrs Graham. 'Here's another noise.' This time the children could hear some jingling. What do you think it was?

Jesus met two men who couldn't see. They had to listen hard all the time because they were blind.

Read the story of how Jesus helped the blind men in Matthew 20:29-34.

Play the listening game for a few moments. Close your eyes and listen hard. What things can you hear? Open your eyes. Did you guess right?

Lord Jesus, thank you for giving me eyes to see. Thank you for helping two men who couldn't see. Please help me to be a good helper too. Amen.

Ten men

Mrs Graham had made a display of things for the children at playgroup to touch.

Amy ran her fingers over a lumpy yam. Then she picked up a prickly fir cone. She touched her own hand and stroked her skin. 'I'm smooth,' she said. Then she looked at her knee. There was a scab on it. 'But not all over!'

Jesus met some men – but they didn't have smooth skin. Their skins were covered in sore places. They had a skin disease. It meant they were not allowed to live in their own homes. They had to stay outside the town so that other people wouldn't catch it. Find out how Jesus helped them in Luke 17:11-19.

Colour in how many men remembered to say 'Thank you' to Jesus.

Today, doctors know much more about helping people with skin diseases. And Jesus still wants to help people in need too.

Lord Jesus, thank you for helping ten men who needed to be made well. Please help me to be a good helper too. Amen.

Hungry people

'Mum, is there something I can eat?' Ben had just got home from school and was feeling hungry.

'You can have some fruit from the bowl,' replied mum. What do you think Ben will choose?

Jesus met some people who were very hungry. They had been listening to him all day. Now it was evening time, and they had no food to eat.

Read the story in Luke 9:10-17 and find out how Jesus helped them.

Draw what he gave the people to eat.

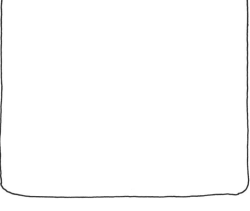

Lord Jesus, thank you for helping a crowd of hungry people. Please help me to be a good helper too. Amen.

Jesus thanked God for the food before he gave it to the crowd. Make up a 'thank you' prayer together which your family could use at meal times, or write a 'thank you' song to the tune of a nursery rhyme.

Frightened people

One day, Jesus' friends were frightened. Read about it in Mark 4:35-41.

How did Jesus help them?

'What's the time, Mr Wolf?' 'Dinner time!' called Mrs Graham as she turned to catch the children. The boys and girls ran away, screaming and laughing.

Most of the children loved running away from Mrs Graham as she tried to catch them. But a new boy called Sean began to cry.

'Stand still,' said Mrs Graham, 'and be quiet. Sean is frightened.'

Lord Jesus, thank you for helping your friends when they were frightened. Please help me to be a good helper too. Amen.

Here's a game to play after reading the story. One person pretends to be the wind (making 'Oooo!' noises) and the waves (waving arms about). The other calls, 'Storm is rising! ... getting rougher ... getting louder!' Then he says, 'Jesus said, 'Be still!'. At once, the first person must be still and quiet. The game could then be repeated, with the players changing places.

At the wedding

Jesus went to a wedding party where the drink ran out. John 2:1-11 will tell you about it.

Can you find the six jars hidden in this picture?

Mrs Graham was arranging a party for the King Street playgroup. Annie and Marcus were helping her to get everything ready.

Mrs Graham was just pouring out the drinks when she gasped, 'Oh no,! I've run out of fruit juice. There won't be enough for everyone!'

'We'll have to buy some more before the party starts,' said Annie. 'It won't be a very good party if we run out of drink.'

Lord Jesus, thank you for helping the people who wanted their party to be a good one. Please help me to be a good helper too. Amen.

Jesus wants us to help too

The King Street playgroup party was great! But when it was over, there was a lot of clearing up to do.

'Who's going to do all this work?' asked Marcus.

'We will,' said his mum. 'If we all help, it won't take long. You can collect the cups and take them to the kitchen, Marcus.'

'Can't I go home with David instead?' asked Marcus.

What do you think Marcus should do? Try to make up a good ending to the story of Marcus and the party.

Now look back and read your favourite 'Jesus the helper' story again.

Lord Jesus, thank you for helping so many different people. Please help me to be a good helper too. Amen.

Make some sugar mice for a party

You will need:

450g icing sugar (sifted)

I egg white

some liquorice lace

4 chocolate buttons halved

a few drops of food colouring

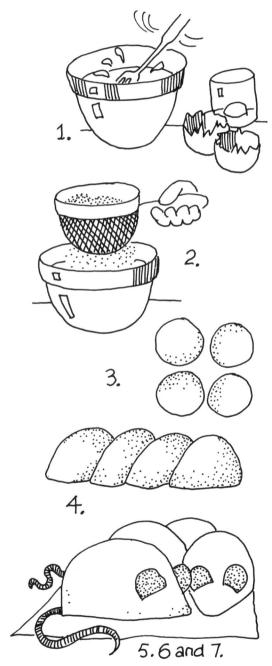

1.

2.

3.

4.

5. 6 and 7.

- Whisk the egg white slightly with the food colouring.
- Add the sifted icing sugar. Mix them together to make a stiff mixture.
- Divide the mixture into four pieces.
- Shape each piece to look like a mouse.
- Use the halved chocolate buttons to make ears.
- Use the liquorice to make tails.
- Leave your mice to harden on some greaseproof paper.

Meet Jacob's family

Some twins look alike, but Esau and Jacob didn't. You can find out how different they were by reading Genesis 25:24-26. (Now can you work out which twin is which?)

Meet Kim and Mark Wong. They were born on the same day, so they're twins!

When Esau and Jacob grew up, they enjoyed different things. Look at Genesis 25:27,28 to find out what each twin liked to do.

Prayer time

Draw a picture of each person in your family and show how you are all different. Point to each picture in turn and say 'thank you' to God for every person.

There's a story in the Bible about twins. They were twin boys, Esau and Jacob. Their parents, Isaac and Rebecca were very proud of their sons.

Jacob cheats his brother

It was time for Isaac to give his elder son all that he owned. This should have been Esau because he was just a few minutes older than Jacob. It meant that Esau would become more important than Jacob.

The Bible tells us that Rebecca, Jacob's mother, wasn't pleased about that. She wanted Jacob, not Esau, to have everything that Isaac owned.

Rebecca told Jacob to play a trick on his father. He dressed up and pretended to be Esau (Genesis 27:1-28).

Do you think that was a good thing to do?

God doesn't want us to cheat each other or play nasty tricks. He knows that it's better to be kind to one another. That way, everyone ends up being happy!

Lord God, please teach us to be kind to each other, so that we will always be a happy family. Amen.

Jacob runs away

Rebecca must have been very sad to say 'goodbye' to Jacob. But she knew that Laban would look after him.

When Esau found out about Jacob's trick, he was furious! He was so angry with Jacob that he wanted to kill Jacob.

Rebecca found out about Esau's plan. 'Jacob,' she said, 'Esau is very angry with you. You must run away. Go and stay with your Uncle Laban's family for a while. You will be safe there.' (Genesis 27:42-45)

Talk to God about the times you say 'goodbye' to people.

Jacob has a dream

'I had a funny dream last night,' Amy told the family one morning. 'I dreamed I was riding on a big pink balloon and looking down on everyone in King Street!'

Sometimes dreams are funny or just silly or even a bit frightening.

When Jacob was travelling to see his uncle Laban, he had a dream. It wasn't funny or silly or frightening. It was a dream that God gave him because he had something important to say to Jacob. You can read about it in Genesis 28:10-22.

God loved Jacob. Although Jacob had done wrong, God still loved him. He wanted Jacob to know that he would never leave him.

Father God, we know that you love us and will never leave us. Thank you. Amen.

Jacob's new job

'When I grow up,' said Ben, 'I'm going to be a postman like Dad.'

'And I'm going to work in the optician's like Mum,' said David.

Amy thought hard. Then she looked at Robbie. 'I want a job looking after animals,' Amy decided.

What job would you like?

When Jacob arrived at Uncle Laban's, he was given a job looking after his uncle's animals. You can find out what animals they were and how Jacob met his uncle by reading Genesis 29:1-14.

Prayer time

Think about some of the jobs done by people you know. Say 'thank you' to God for what they do to help you.

Make a 'Jobs' book or poster with your child. Find pictures from papers or magazines to stick in it. Help your child to understand how some of the jobs help us.

Jacob goes home

The last time Jacob had seen Esau, Esau had wanted to kill Jacob (Genesis 27:41). So Jacob asked God to help him.

While Jacob was living at his Uncle Laban's, he got married.

After a long time, Jacob decided to go back to his own country. With him he took two of his cousins, his eleven sons, his daughter and lots of servants.

He even took four kinds of animals. Can you find three of them in this picture?

When I am worried, Father God, help me to remember that you can help me. Amen.

Jacob meets Esau

As Jacob travelled home, he wondered whether Esau was still angry with him. He heard that Esau was coming to meet him, so he sent him some presents to show that he wanted to be friends.

As Jacob came close to Esau, he bowed down to show Esau that he didn't want to fight him. Read about their meeting in Genesis 33:3-5.

What a happy ending to the story! The brothers had quarrelled, but now they were friends.

Think about some happy times you have had with your family. Talk to God about them.

If you have photographs of happy family events, get them out to help your child recall what happened. Try to find out what it is that you child enjoys most about these happy occasions.

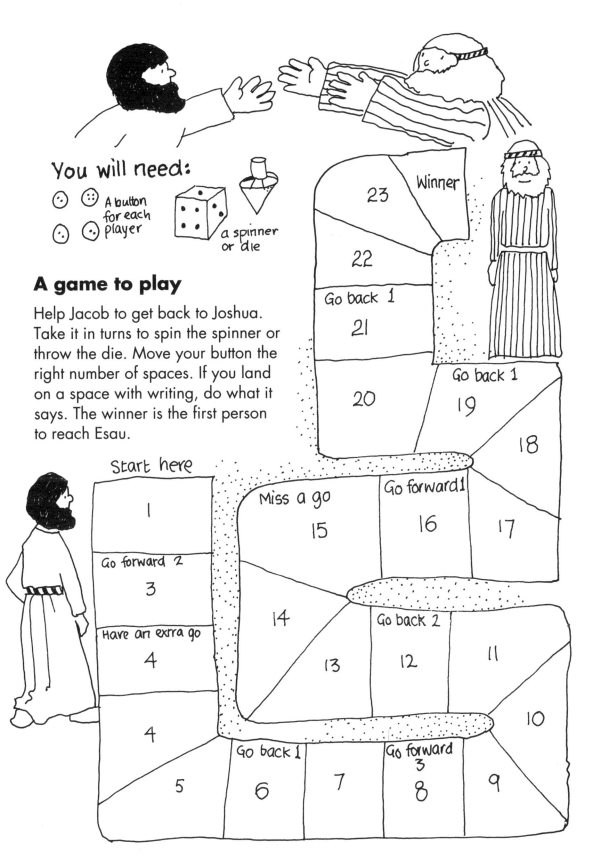

You will need:

A button for each player

a spinner or die

A game to play

Help Jacob to get back to Joshua. Take it in turns to spin the spinner or throw the die. Move your button the right number of spaces. If you land on a space with writing, do what it says. The winner is the first person to reach Esau.

Start here

1

Go forward 2
3

Have an extra go
4

4

5

Go back 1
6

7

Go forward 3
8

9

10

11

Go back 2
12

13

14

Miss a go
15

Go forward 1
16

17

18

Go forward 1
19

Go back 1

20

Go back 1
21

22

23

Winner

PARENTS For the next few days, we will be looking at God's creation. The prayer times will come from Psalm 148, which is printed here. Read it through beforehand with your child. Then each day, help them to find the verses which make up the prayer. Encourage them to join in with the words 'Praise the Lord'.

Psalm 148 Praise the Lord!

Praise the Lord from heaven, you that live in the height above. Praise him, all his angels, all his heavenly armies.

Praise him, sun and moon; praise him, shining stars. Praise him, highest heavens, and the waters above the sky.

Let them all praise the name of the Lord! He commanded, and they were created; by his commands they were fixed in their places for ever, and they cannot disobey.

Praise the Lord from the earth, sea-monsters and all ocean depths; lightning and hail, snow and clouds, strong winds that obey his command.

Praise him, hills and mountains, fruit trees and forests; all animals, tame and wild, reptiles and birds.

Praise him, kings and all peoples, princes and other rulers; girls and young men, old people and children too.

Let them all praise the name of the Lord! His name is greater than all others; his glory is above earth and heaven. He made his nation strong, so that all his people praise him – the people of Israel, so dear to him .

Praise the Lord!

Earth

Amy and Kim were playing in the back garden. 'Let's do some digging,' suggested Amy.

They found some seaside spades in the shed and began to dig in the soft, brown earth.

'Nothing's growing here,' said Amy.

'It's just an empty place,' agreed Kim.

Read Genesis 1:9,10.

When God made the earth, it was empty at first – no plants, no animals, no people. But God was pleased with what he'd made. He knew that it was a place where things would be able to live and grow.

Our earth is a good place to live. God made it for us.

Praise the Lord! Praise him girls and young men, old people and children too. Praise the Lord!

Cultivate a new patch of garden, window box or some indoor plants with your child. Let him or her enjoy 'creating' a garden and watching it grow.

Water

'Mum, can we plant some seeds in that empty patch of earth?' asked Amy. 'Yes – shall I buy some for you when I go shopping?' said mum.

So Mrs Miller brought some seeds for the girls. But when Kim came round to help plant them, it started to rain hard.

'Stupid rain!' shouted Kim. 'Now we can't go outside!'

'I wish it didn't ever rain,' grumbled Amy.

'You couldn't grow a garden if it never rained,' Mrs Miller reminded them. 'Your seeds need water to help them grow. And the rain is making the soil ready for the seeds.'

Read Genesis 1:6-9.

When God made the water, he knew how important it was. Water helps plants to grow – but what else do we need water for? Think of some ideas.

Praise the Lord! Praise him, highest heavens and the waters above the sky. Praise the Lord, lightning and hail, snow and clouds. Praise the Lord!

Sun, moon and stars

It had been a rainy day. Amy looked out of the window at bed time. The sky was clear now. 'Look at the moon!' she cried out. 'It's really big and bright!'

Ben came to look. 'So are the stars.' he said. 'I can see hundreds of them!'

How many stars can you find?

Dad came to look out of the window too. 'What a beautiful sky tonight,' he agreed. 'If the sky is as clear tomorrow, Amy, the sun will be shining. And you can start your garden.'

Read Genesis 1:14-18.

God made the sun to give the earth warmth and light. He made the moon and the stars to shine when it's dark.

Praise the Lord!
Praise him, sun and moon;
Praise him, shining stars.
Praise the Lord!

25

Plants

Genesis 1:11,12 says that when God made the earth, he filled it with plants of all kinds. There were flowers, trees, grasses, vegetables, bushes of all sizes and all colours. God has made a wonderful world for us to enjoy.

'We can start our garden today,' said Amy. Kim came round to help. Kim carried the seed packets into the back garden.

Dad showed them how to rake the bare soil and sprinkle the seeds over it.

'This place won't be empty for much longer,' said Kim.

'No,' said Mr Miller, 'One day it will be full of beautiful flowers and plants.'

Colour the pictures on the seed packets.

Praise the Lord! Praise him hills and mountains, fruit trees and forests. Praise the Lord!

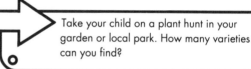

Take your child on a plant hunt in your garden or local park. How many varieties can you find?

Animals

When God made the earth, he created all kinds of creatures – birds, insects, fish, land animals and sea animals (Genesis 1:20-25). Draw your favourite creature here:

Amy and Kim's seeds were beginning to grow - but so were the weeds! Amy found some long, green leaves. 'That's a dandelion,' she said. 'Better pull it up. It's a weed.'

'Give it to me,' replied Kim. 'I'll take it home for Bugsy to eat. He loves dandelions.'

Amy thought about Bugsy. 'I like your rabbit,' she said, 'because he's small and soft to stroke.'

Praise the Lord! Praise him all animals, tame and wild, reptiles and birds. Praise the Lord!

Find some pictures of animals. Glue them on to a large piece of paper to make a poster. Write today's prayer on it.

People

Find some pictueres of flowers. Stick them in this space to make a colourful garden like Amy and Kim's.

At last Amy and Kim's flowers grew and opened. They looked beautiful!

Kim's family came to admire the garden. Amy and Kim were very pleased with it.

Amy and Kim were glad that they had looked after their garden.

Read Genesis 1:26-27.

When God made the earth, he created people to look after it and to enjoy what he had made. People are special because we are able to look after God's world. We can thank God for all the lovely things around us.

Praise the Lord! Praise him, girls and young men, old people and children too. Let them all praise the name of the Lord!

All creation

God made everything in the world! How many different things can you find in this picture?

The story of God's creation is in Genesis 1:1-2:3. Ask someone to read it to you.

Prayer time

Look back at Psalm 148. Use your favourite verses to help you praise God for his wonderful creation.

EASTER

PARENTS →
These pictures tell the Easter story in brief. Parts of it are very sad, so read it all with your child before going on to the next section of readings. Fill in the details afterwards by reading or retelling the Bible verses.

1 Jesus decided to go to Jerusalem. He rode on a donkey. All the people cheered him! **Matthew 21:1-9**

2 But some people hated Jesus. They were afraid of what he might do. **Matthew 26:3-5**

3 Jesus knew that he was going to die. He ate a 'goodbye' meal with his friends. He promised to come back. **Matthew 26:17-19, 26-30**

4 After the meal, Jesus and his friends went to a quiet garden. Jesus talked to God.
Matthew 26:36-39

5 Jesus' enemies sent a crowd of men to take Jesus away. His friends were frightened and ran away.
Matthew 26:47-56

6 Jesus' friends were very sad because Jesus had died. They thought they would never see him again. **Matthew 27:55-61**

7 Some women who loved Jesus, went to see where Jesus' body had been put. **Matthew 28:1**

8 An angel told them, 'He is not here. He is alive again!'
Matthew 28:2-7

9 The women went back to tell everyone. On the way they met Jesus himself. He really was alive!
Matthew 28:8-9

10 Jesus met all his friends again. 'I will never leave you,' he said. 'I'll always be with my friends.'
Matthew 28:16-20

Jesus goes to Jerusalem

When Jesus went into Jerusalem, he wanted everyone to be able to see him. What did he ride on? Look at Matthew 21:6,7.

Amy was looking out of the window. She saw all the cars whizzing up and down King Street.

'I want to see who's driving – a man or a lady,' she told Mum. 'But they are going so fast I can't tell.'

'If you were going to ride up King Street so that everyone could see you,' said Mum, 'what would you ride in?'

'Something slower,' said Amy. 'And something that I could ride on top of instead of inside. Then people would notice me.'

The people who saw him knew that Jesus was special. They shouted, 'God bless him who comes in the name of the Lord! Praise God!'

Jesus is special. Here are some words to praise him. 'Jesus is our friend! He's our King! Praise God!'

32

Jesus has enemies

Ben was looking at his Bible picture book. 'Why have those people got angry faces?' he asked.

Dad had a look. 'This is a sad story,' he told Ben. 'Jesus was always kind and loving and he had many friends. But some people hated Jesus.'

'Why?' asked Ben, very surprised.

It is hard to understand this part of Jesus' story. But some people hated Jesus so much that they wanted to kill him.

It's wonderful, though, to remember that Jesus is alive today. He did die, but he came alive again!

Lord Jesus, we love you. We are glad that you are alive again. Amen.

Matthew 26:6-13 is about the woman who poured perfume over Jesus feet. Read it and explain to your child that, although some people hated Jesus, others, like this woman, went on loving him.

A special meal

Uncle Ross was going to live far away in another country, so the Millers were having a special meal to say goodbye.

Ben, Amy and David were sad. Even Robbie, the dog, looked gloomy!

'We'll never see you again!' said David.

'Yes, you will,' Uncle Ross told them. 'I'll be back to see you one day.'

Amy asked, 'You won't forget about us?'

'No,' promised Uncle Ross, 'I'll think about you all the time.'

Jesus had to say 'goodbye' to his friends. They were very sad and so was Jesus. But he promised, 'I will see you again.'

What did Jesus and his friends eat and drink at the special 'goodbye' meal? Matthew 26:26-29 will tell you.

Draw the food and drink here.

Thank you, Lord Jesus, that I will never have to say goodbye to you. You are always with me. Amen.

Jesus talks to God

Jesus had something hard to do so he talked to God about it. He took his friends to a quiet garden. He told God how he felt.

It would have been easier for Jesus to go home. But he said he would do whatever God wanted, however hard it was.

It was a cold, wet morning. Mr Miller got up early to go to work. David got up early too.

'Why don't you stay at home?' he asked as Dad put on his postman's coat.

'I can't,' he replied. 'It would be easier to stay warm and dry at home, but people are waiting for their letters. I've got to go and deliver them.'

When I have hard things to do, Lord God, help me to be brave and patient, just like Jesus was. Amen.

Jesus is arrested

Amy and David were out shopping with their mum. Suddenly, a big dog began barking behind a fence.

Amy squealed and David burst into tears. Even Mrs Miller gave a jump. And they all began to run as fast as they could! They were scared!

'I thought that dog was going to hurt us!' said Amy.

'I'm glad Robbie's a nice, friendly dog,' gasped David.

When Jesus and his friends were in the quiet garden, a crowd of men, sent by Jesus' enemies, came to take Jesus away. Jesus' friends were frightened. Every one of them ran away. Only Jesus was not scared. He knew that God was with him.

Talk about times when you are frightened. Then remember that God is always there to help. Say 'thank you' to him.

Jesus dies

When Jesus died on a cross, his friends were very, very sad. They thought they would never see him again, but they were wrong!

They had forgotten his promise. Can you remember what it was?

Mrs Miller works in an opticians. One day she came home from work looking sad. 'Miss Phillips has died. We used to make spectacles for her,' she explained.

'Was she a nice lady?' asked Ben.

'Yes,' said mum. 'She was always making us laugh. I'm sorry I won't be seeing her again.'

They were going to have such a wonderful surprise!

I will see you again

Father God, thank you that Jesus' story has a happy ending. When I am sad, help me to remember that you still love me. Amen.

If your child has known someone (or had a pet) who has died, take time to talk this over. Explain that, normally, people who die do not come back to life. It is a very special and wonderful thing that Jesus came back to life again.

Jesus is alive!

The Miller family went to church on Easter Sunday. Dr and Mrs Graham were there with Annie and Marcus.

'Happy Easter!' called Dr Graham with a big smile. 'Happy Easter!' called Mrs Graham and the children happily.

'Why are they so happy today?' asked David. 'Is it because they've had lots of Easter eggs?'

What do you think?
Matthew 28:1-9 will help you find out why people are happy at Easter time.

Jesus is alive! Say 'thank you' to God for this.

> Even if it is not Easter time, make an Easter garden with your child. Use a waterproof dish or box filled with damp soil or sand. Add moss, small plants and some flowers, either real or paper. Use stones to represent the empty tomb.

Jesus is always with us

Mr Miller walked with David all the way to the King Street playgroup. 'Don't go, dad I want you to stay with me,' David said at the door.

But Dad couldn't stop. He had to go to work. He waved goodbye to David and hurried off.

'Don't worry, David,' said Mrs Graham. 'I'll be with you until your mum comes to collect you.'

David found out that nobody could be with him all the time. Dad had to go to work, so Mrs Graham would look after him until his mum came to collect him.

But Jesus is always with us (Matthew 28:20). He promised that he would never leave us. We can't see him, but we know that he's there, loving us and ready to listen when we talk to him.

Thank you, Lord Jesus, that you are always with me, Amen.

➡ Make a game of learning together Jesus' promise at the end of Matthew 28:20. You say, 'Jesus said, 'I will be ...' and help your child complete it with the words, '...with you always'.

39

You will need:

some felt tipped pens

some greaseproof paper

some black card

glue

scissors

Make a stained glass window

• Trace the picture onto greaseproof paper.

• Colour it in with felt tipped pens (draw the lines in black).

• Ask someone to cut out two squares of card, slightly larger than your picture.

• Ask someone to help you cut a hole, the same size as your picture, in the middle of both pieces of card.

• Cut out your picture, leaving a border of paper all the way round it.

• Glue your picture to one piece of card so that it shows through the hole.

• Glue the two pieces of card together. Put your 'stained glass' by a window so that the light can shine through.

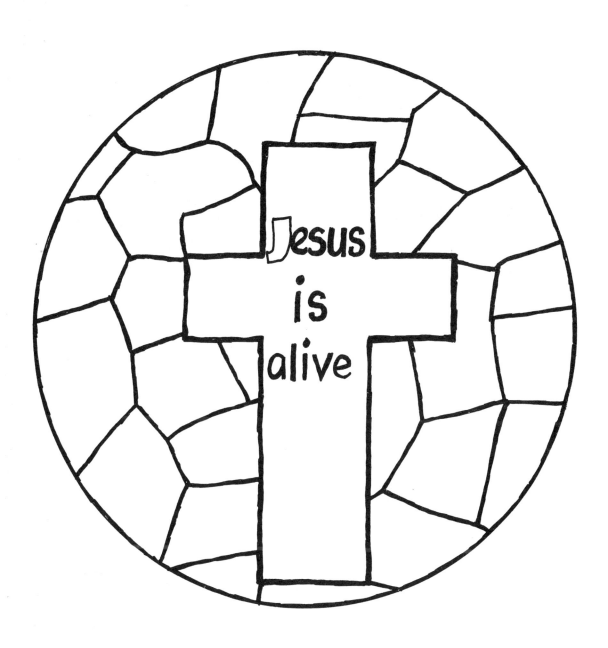

Jesus shows us how

The people who go to King Street church on Sundays always say this special prayer together.

Our Father in heaven: May your holy name be honoured; may your Kingdom come; may your will be done on earth as it is in heaven. Give us today the food we need. Forgive us all the wrongs we have done, as we forgive the wrongs that others have done to us. Do not bring us to hard testing, but keep us safe from the Evil One. (Matthew 6:9-11)

It's called the Lord's prayer because the Lord Jesus taught it to his friends. He wanted to show them what sort of things they could talk to God about.

It doesn't matter what words you use when you talk to God. You don't have to say long, difficult words when you pray. God is pleased whatever you want to say.

What would you like to say to God? Talk to him now.

Help your child to learn the Lord's prayer during this section of readings. Either use the version above (from the Good News Bible) or the version used in your church. Your child's feeling of belonging will increase as he or she enjoys being able to say the prayer with other people in the church community.

Our Father in heaven

Amy knows that Mrs Miller's name is Helen and Mr Miller's name is Bob. 'What's God's name?' she asked.

Do you ever wonder that? The Bible gives us lots of names for God, but Jesus says we can call God 'Our Father'.

Who looks after you? Think about all the good things that are done for you by that person.

Just like a good parent, God loves us and cares for us. He gives us all the things we really need and keeps us safe. That is why Jesus taught us to call him 'Our Father'.

Make up a prayer to God which begins 'Our Father...'.

43

May your Kingdom come

Mr Miller likes collecting stamps. He has stamps from countries all round the world which he sticks in a big album. He put all the stamps from the same country together.

Colour in these stamps.

Ben was watching Dad looking at the words on each stamp to find out which country it came from.

But some stamps had no writing on. 'Where are they from?' asked Ben.

'From the United Kingdom,' answered Dad.

'What's a Kingdom?' asked Ben.

'It's a country where the people have a king or queen to rule over them,' explained Dad.

God wants to be our King. But his Kingdom isn't a country. Wherever people love God and try to please him, that's where God's Kingdom is.

When we say the Lord's prayer, we are asking God to make his Kingdom come in our homes.

Our Father, we want you as our King. May your Kingdom come in our home today. Amen.

Your will be done

We know that he wants us to be helpful and kind and friendly. So when we do those things, we are doing God's will. And God has promised to help us.

'Mum, can I do anything to help you?' asked David.

Mrs Miller thought for a moment. 'I know,' she said, 'I want to make some sandwiches for lunch. You could help me butter the bread.'

In the Lord's prayer, we say, 'Our Father ... your will be done.' This means that we want to find out the things that God wants us to do.

Our Father, we want to do what you want. May your will be done in our home today. Amen.

The food we need

What is your favourite food? Draw it here.

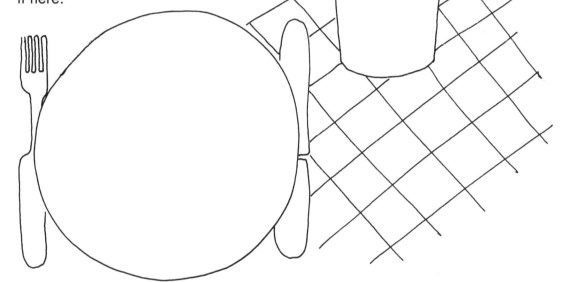

In the Lord's prayer, we say, 'Give us today the food we need.' We are asking God for enough food to keep us healthy and fit.

That may mean we can't always have our favourite food. We need to have other foods too so that we will grow up to be strong and well.

Prayer time

Our Father, we thank you for all the good food that you have provided for us to enjoy. Amen.

As a way of thanking God for the food he gives us, why not arrange a special meal this week which includes some of your family's favourite food?

Forgive us

When Mrs Miller went away for a few days, she promised to bring back some presents for the children.

But when she came back, there were no presents. 'I just didn't have time,' she said. 'I am very sorry.'

'Never mind, mum,' said Amy. 'We're just glad that you're home. We missed you very much.'

It's not always easy to say 'sorry' or to forgive other people, but that is what God wants us to do.

When we say the Lord's prayer, we ask God to forgive us for the wrong things we have done. And the prayer also reminds us to forgive other people who have upset us.

Our Father, forgive us all the wrongs we have done, as we forgive the wrongs that others have done to us. Amen.

Keep us safe

David was usually very happy in the day time, but sometimes at night he felt afraid.

'Stay with me,' he asked Mum and Dad.

But they couldn't. 'What makes you feel afraid?' they asked him.

David didn't know, so Mum and Dad taught him to say part of the Lord's prayer. They knew that God could help David feel safe, even when he was alone.

God doesn't want us to be afraid or harmed. So when we talk to God we can say, 'Keep us safe'.

Make a poster like David's for your bedroom wall.

Ask God to keep you safe wherever you go and whatever you are doing.

We can talk to God

There are lots of ways to talk to God! Here are some you could try.

• Picture prayers

Cut out or draw pictures of some things you want to thank God for. You could glue them onto some paper to make a 'Thank you, God' poster.

• Finishing prayers

Someone could a start a prayer for other people to finish in their own way. Everyone should try to have their own way of ending the prayer.

• Psalm prayers

There are lots of prayers in the Bible book of Psalms. Here are some which your family might enjoy: Psalm 8; Psalm 65:9-13; Psalm 67; Psalm 150. Sing them, shout them, clap to them, enjoy them!

Remember, God loves to hear you talking to him.

Our Father, we are glad that you want us to talk to you. Today we want to say .....

You will need:

two pieces of card about the size of your King Street book

some crayons or pens

a brass split pin

some pictures from magazines

glue

scissors

1.

2.

thank you God for

3.

thank you God for

Make a prayer circle

• Cut out two circles of card. Make them the same size as the circle on the next page.

• Divide one circle into six equal parts. Draw or stick something or someone from God's world in each part. The circle on the next page will give you some ideas.

• Cut a segment-sized section out of the second circle. On it write 'Thank you, God, for..'.

• Use the brass split pin to fix the two circles together.

• Each day, turn to a new section and thank God for his world.

JOSEPH

PARENTS ➡️

For the next few days we will be reading the story of Joseph. Read this picture story with your child first. It gives only the briefest details of the Bible passages, so you may wish to read the Bible verses, then retell the story in your own words.

1 Meet Joseph. His father, Jacob, gave him a special coat. But when Jacob showed off, his brothers got angry. **Genesis 37:1-11**

2 One day, the brothers decided to get rid of Joseph. They put him in a dry pit. **Genesis 37:12-24**

3 Then they sold him to some camel men. When the brothers went home, they told their father that Joseph was dead. **Genesis 37:25-28**

4 Joseph was taken to Egypt. He was sold to Potiphar and had to do whatever Potiphar told him. **Genesis 37:36; 39:1-6**

5 Joseph worked hard, but Potiphar's wife told lies about him. Potiphar was angry and put Joseph in prison. **Genesis 39:19 - 40:23**

6 Joseph worked hard in the prison. One day, he told two men what their dreams meant. One of these was the king's wine steward. 'The king will soon set you free,' Joseph told him. 'When he does, please tell him about me. I want to be free too.' **Genesis 41:1-14**

7 Two years later, the king had a dream. Then the wine steward remembered Joseph. The king's servants fetched Joseph from prison. God helped Joseph to tell the king what his dream meant. Joseph said, 'For seven years, there will be plenty of food. After that, for seven more years, no food will grow.'
Genesis 41:15-36

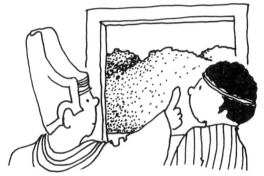

8 The king was pleased with Joseph. He put Joseph in charge of storing the food. **Genesis 41:37-57**

9 When the bad years came, Joseph's brothers came to Egypt to ask for food. They had none at home. At first, Joseph didn't tell them who he was. Then he said, 'I am Joseph, your brother.'
Genesis 42-45

10 The brothers were overjoyed to see Joseph. They came to live in Egypt and the whole family was together again. **Genesis 46 - 47:12**

Joseph shows off

Meet Joseph. He lived in Bible times.

Here's a song to sing or say:

God never stops loving me,
Wherever I may go.
God never stops loving me.
He never stops loving you.
God loves me!

Christine Orme © Scripture Union.

We read about his father, Jacob, earlier in King Street. Joseph also had eleven brothers and a sister. Joseph had a special coat because he was Jacob's favourite son.

Joseph sometimes had dreams. He dreamed about sheaves of corn and about the sun, moon and stars.

Joseph thought that he was more important than his brothers. That made his brothers very angry.

Joseph kept showing off. It made his family very unhappy. But, all the time, God kept loving him.

When I show off and make other people unhappy, please forgive me, Father God. Amen.

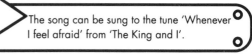

The song can be sung to the tune 'Whenever I feel afraid' from 'The King and I'.

Joseph in trouble

Joseph's brothers were not as ready to be friends with him. Even when they were all grown up, they still hated Joseph. They thought it would be a good idea to get rid of him for ever.

They took off his special robe and threw him into a dry pit. Joseph must have been very sad and frightened, but, all the time, God still loved him.

David had been playing at Mark's house. He came home looking very cross.

'What's wrong?' asked Mum.

'I'm never playing with Mark again!' he shouted.

David and Mark had quarrelled. They thought they'd never want to see each other again. But the next day, they felt better and made friends again!

Father God, it's great to know that you still love me, no matter happens. Amen.

55

Joseph and the camel men

Colour in the shapes with a dot in and find a picture.

When Joseph was in the dry pit, some men came by. They had camels loaded with goods they were taking to a faraway land called Egypt.

Joseph's brothers saw the camel men and made a plan. You can read about their wicked plan in Genesis 37:25-28.

Joseph was made to go away from his family, away from his home, away from his own country. But, all the time, God was still with Joseph. God never stopped loving him.

However we feel, we know that God still loves us. He'll never stop loving us. Say 'thank you' to him for this.

Your child may need some reassurance that his brothers will not do the same thing as Joseph's brothers. Look back at the cartoon story to see how the story ended happily.

Joseph and Potiphar

Here are Ben, Amy and David helping with some jobs. Can you say what they are doing?

What jobs do you help with?

Joseph had a new job in Egypt. Read what he had to do in Potiphar's house in Genesis 39:1-7.

Joseph was a good worker and Potiphar was pleased with him. God was helping Joseph to work hard in everything he did.

Prayer time

Lord God, please help me, in all my work and play, to please you. Amen.

Joseph goes to prison

Ben was painting a picture. Suddenly he knocked the paint pot and paint went all over the carpet! Ben was afraid that he would get told off.

'Who spilt paint on the carpet?' asked Dad.

'David did,' said Ben. 'I didn't!' shouted David.

Dad looked at both of them. 'Who really spilt it?' he asked.

Ben looked at the floor. 'I did,' he muttered, 'It was an accident. I'm sorry.'

Ben told a lie because he was afraid that Dad would be cross with him. But Dad soon forgave him and everything was all right again.

Things didn't go so well for Joseph. Potiphar's wife told lies about him. Potiphar believed that Joseph had done something very wrong. Joseph was put into prison because of the lies.

It was a terrible thing that happened to Joseph, but, all the time, God still loved him.

Whatever happens, whether it's good or bad, you still go on loving me, Father God. I thank you. Amen.

Joseph in prison

One of the people Joseph met in prison was the king's wine steward.

The wine steward had a dream about a grapevine (Genesis 40:9-11). 'I wonder what it means,' he thought.

God helped Joseph to tell the wine steward what his dream meant. 'In three days time,' said Joseph,'you will be allowed out of prison. You will go back to work for the king. When that happens, please try to get me out of prison.'

Three days later, the wine steward was let out of prison. He went back to work for the king, just as Joseph had said. But he forgot all about Joseph and Joseph stayed in prison.

Do you think God had forgotten about Joseph? Of course he hadn't! God never stops loving anyone.

Thank you, Lord God, that you always care about me, whatever happens. Amen.

The king's dream

'Oh dear,' sighed Mrs Miller as she looked out of the window. 'It was so windy last night that some tiles have blown off the roof.'

'Will you put them back?' asked Amy. 'No,' replied her mum, 'I don't know how to. I'll have to ask someone to help me.'

Does your family ever need help?

The king of Egypt needed help. He had had some very strange dreams and he wanted to know what they meant.

The king's wine steward knew who could help the king. Draw over the dots to find out who it was.

Joseph asked God to help him. Then he told the king what the dreams meant. Genesis 41:25-32 will tell you what he said.

Father God, thank you for helping Joseph. Amen.

Joseph's new job

Amy and David like eating bread. But where does bread come from? These pictures tell the story of how bread gets to the shops.

If the grain doesn't grow, then there is no bread!

Joseph told the king of Egypt that there would be lots of grain for seven years, but then no grain would grow for another seven years. The king needed to store grain ready to use when nothing was growing.

The king of Egypt chose someone to be in charge of storing the grain properly. Can you guess who it was? Genesis 41:37-43 will tell you.

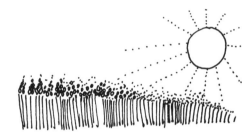

Father God, thank you for all the people who make sure that we have enough to eat. Amen.

Make a food montage using labels from cans, panels from food packets, and pictures of food. Use it as a basis for thanking God for all the food he has given us.

Joseph and his brothers

Do you remember Joseph's brothers? They had planned to kill Joseph, but God had kept him safe.

Now the brothers were older – and they were very hungry. There was no food in their country because no grain was growing.

When the brothers heard that there was food in Egypt they decided to go there to buy some.

Get the brothers to Egypt.

When the brothers met Joseph in Egypt, they didn't know who he was! Joseph looked very different, but he was still their brother.

Something else was different too. God had helped Joseph to change the way he behaved. Joseph didn't want to show off to his brothers any more. Instead, he wanted to be kind to them. He said, 'Come and live in Egypt where there's plenty of food. Then you and your families won't be hungry.'

Ask God to help you do kind things for people, and not unkind things.

Spend time talking about the ways people change, both in looks and in character.

Together again!

What is your family happy about at the moment?

Sing or say:
    God never stops loving me,
    Wherever I may go.
    God never stops loving me.
    He never stops loving you.
    God loves me!

Use these words from Psalm 105: 2,3 to praise God. 'Sing praise to the Lord: tell of the wonderful things he has done. Be glad that we belong to him; let all who worship him rejoice.'

God loved Joseph and his family all the time they were away from each other. At the end of this Bible story about Joseph's family, God brought them back together after their sad years apart.

    They were very happy to see each other again! Draw all their happy faces here.

A servant girl

Ben was helping mum in the kitchen. Amy came in. 'Can I help?' she asked.

'No!' said Ben, 'You're only four. You're too little!'

'Wait a minute,' said mum, 'You don't have to be big or grown up to be helpful. Amy can help us too.'

Naaman was an important man. He was a great soldier who lived in Bible times. But Naaman didn't know about God.

There was someone living in Naaman's house who was going to help him find out about God. It was a little girl. She was a servant who helped Naaman's wife, but God chose her to help Naaman, too.

Here's a rhyme to say together as you share the story of Naaman:

Finding out
All about
God and his love.
Look and see
Just how he
Wants us to live.

Thank you, Father God, that children are so important to you. Amen.

Elisha could help

Finding out
All about
God and his love.
Look and see
Just how he
Wants us to live.

Naaman had a problem! He had a terrible skin disease. None of the doctors could make him well. The skin disease just get worse and worse.

Naaman didn't know what to do! He didn't know about God and how he could help. But someone did! Can you guess who? Read the story in 2 Kings 5:1-5.

The little servant girl was helping Naaman to find out just how great God is.

'O Lord, my God, how great you are! As long as I live, I will sing praise to my God.' Psalm 104:1,33

Naaman goes on a journey

Ben, David, Amy and Robbie the dog were playing in the garden. They were pretending to go on a long journey to find hidden treasure!

Naaman set off on his journey to Israel. He hoped that he'd find someone to cure his disease. He even took presents to pay for it (2 Kings 5:5,6).

Naaman didn't know about God. He didn't understand that we don't need to pay God for helping us. God loves us so much that he wants to give us everything we need.

> Finding out
> All about
> God and his love.
> Look and see
> Just how he
> Wants us to live.

O Lord, you are a great God. You know what we need and are always ready to show us your love. Amen.

Naaman sees the king

The king was an important person, but he couldn't make Naaman better. Only God could do that. Naaman still had to find out how great God is!

Who helps you when you are ill? Write their names or draw them here.

Finding out
All about
God and his love.
Look and see
Just how he
Wants us to live.

Naaman travelled all the way to Israel. He was hoping to find someone who could make him better. Find out who he went to see by reading 2 Kings 5:7-8.

Prayer time

Lord God, thank you for always helping us. We want to learn more about you too. Amen.

Elisha can help

Meet Elisha.

Elisha had a special job. He told people the things God wanted to say to them. Sometimes God showed Elisha how to help people in special ways.

Elisha was the person who could help Naaman.

Get Naaman to Elisha's house.

The little servant girl had known that God would show Elisha the best way to help Naaman.

Finding out
All about
God and his love.
Look and see
Just how he
Wants us to live.

Thank you, Father God, that you are able to show people the best way to help others. Amen.

Naaman meets Elisha

God showed Elisha what Naaman needed to do to be cured from his skin disease. But Naaman didn't want to do it. Read 2 Kings 5:9-12 to find out about it.

Amy was ill. She had an ear infection. The doctor had given her some medicine to help her get better.

But Amy didn't like the medicine. 'It tastes horrible!' she said, 'I don't want to take it.'

'If you don't take it, you won't get better quickly,' said Dad.

What do you think Amy should do?

Naaman was finding out that we need to do what God says, even when we don't want to. He's such a great God and he always knows best.

Finding out
All about
God and his love.
Look and see
Just how he
Wants us to live.

Lord God, when it's hard to do what you say, please help me. Amen.

Naaman is made better

Amy's ear was getting better. She did what the doctor said and took her medicine, even though it didn't taste very nice.

Elisha didn't give Naaman any medicine. He told him to do something different. Naaman had to wash in the River Jordan.

Read 2 Kings 5:13-15 to find out what happened.

Naaman had found out how great God is! He knows what is best for us and wants us to obey him.

Finding out
All about
God and his love.
Look and see
Just how he
Wants us to live.

'O Lord, my God, how great you are! As long as I live I will sing praises to my God' (Psalm 104:1,33)

You will need:

some card

scissors

a piece of garden cane

some wool

glue   crayons or pencils

Make a sad and happy mask

- Cut a circle out of the card.
- On one side, draw a sad face. Colour it in.
- On the other side, draw a happy face. Colour it in.
- Glue the wool to the top of the faces to make hair.
- Split the garden cane slightly. Slot the face into the cane. Use your mask when you are reading King Street to show if the people in the story are happy or sad.

1.

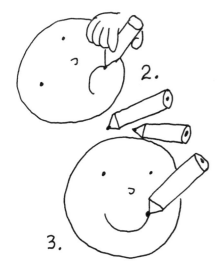

2.

3.

4.

5.

...when I'm happy

The Millers were on holiday. They were staying on a sheep farm and the farmer was a shepherd.

'The sheep are happy today,' she told the family. 'They've got everything they need – a field of grass, fresh water, and sunny weather.'

Read Psalm 23:1-4. It was written a long time ago by a shepherd called David.

God cares for us like a shepherd cares for her sheep. He knows when we are happy – and that makes him glad!

Think about something that makes you happy. Say 'thank you' to God for it.

Take your children to see someone looking after sheep or any other kind of animal. Remind your child that God knows us and cares for us in the same way.

...when I'm sad

Ben was looking round the farm. One of the sheep was in a pen on her own. 'She looks sad,' said Ben.

'I know' said the shepherd. 'She's not very well. I've put her close to the house where I can look after her. I'm giving her some medicine. She'll soon be fit and strong again.'

Draw a sad face. Who helps you to feel better when you are sad?

Read Psalm 23:1-4.

When we are sad, God knows all about it. He understands how we feel, just like a shepherd understands her sheep.

Our Father God, when we are sad, you know about it. Thank you for caring for us.

...when I'm cross

Ben was cross. Mum and Dad had told him that they would be going out for the day. But Ben wanted to stay on the farm to watch the shepherd working.

'It's not fair!' he said to the shepherd.

'Sometimes my sheep get cross like you are today,' she told him.

'Do they?' he asked. 'Why?'

'It's usually when I'm dipping them. I have to make them swim through some cold, smelly water.

The water has something in it to help them stay well. They hate it! But I know what's best for them. If I didn't dip them, they might get very ill.'

Read Psalm 23:1-4.

We get cross when something happens that we don't like. God knows how we feel and he understands.

Have you been cross today? Tell God what it was about, and say 'sorry' to him if you have made other people cross too.

...when I'm sorry

'Go on, Sam.'

Ben was watching the shepherd's dog round up the sheep. Suddenly, one sheep ran away from the rest and squeezed through the hedge.

Help Sam get the sheep back to the shepherd.

Sheep don't always do what the shepherd wants.

Read Psalm 23:1-4.

We don't always do what God wants either. But God doesn't stop loving us. When we do wrong things, he wants to forgive us. So we can say 'sorry' to God and ask him to help us do what is right.

I am sorry,
Father God,
when I am
unkind or rude or
don't obey.
Please forgive
me and help me
do what's right.
Amen.

...when I'm frightened

Read Psalm 23:1-4.

Have you ever been frightened? It's good to remember that, however we feel, God is looking after us just as a shepherd looks after her sheep.

'Baa! Baa!' cried the lamb.

'Is he frightened?' asked Ben.

'Yes,' said the shepherd, 'He wants to be with his mother. But I had to bring him here because he hurt his foot. I had to clean the cut. But he needn't worry. I'll look after him until he's able to go back to her.'

'I will not be afraid, Lord, for you are with me.' Psalm 23:4.

Make some sheep

You
will
need:

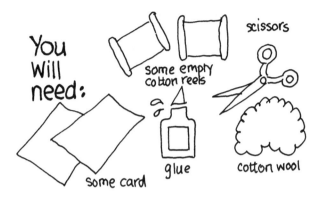

some empty
cotton reels

scissors

glue

cotton wool

some card

- Trace the sheep shapes onto the card. You will need a back and a front for each cotton reel.
- Cut the shapes out and glue some cotton wool onto them.
- Glue some cotton wool around the cotton reel.
- Stick the sheep front onto one end of the cotton reel and the sheep back onto the other end.

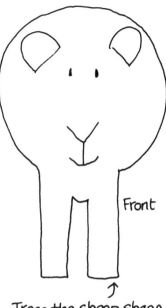

Front

Trace the sheep shape

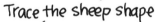

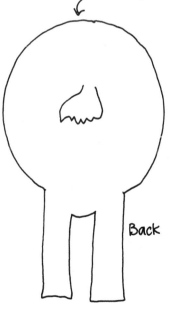

Back

...All about me!

'Look, Ben,' called the shepherd, 'there's the lamb that hurt his foot. Can you see him on the far side of the field by the trees?'

Ben looked hard. 'Which one? All the lambs look the same to me.'

'Not to me,' laughed the shepherd. 'I know them all. Each one is special to me.'

The shepherd knew each one of her sheep. The Bible tells us that God knows all about each one of us. He loves us and knows how we feel. He'll never stop caring about us!

Make a sheep poster to help you remember how much God cares about you. Write your favourite verse from Psalm 23:1-4 on the poster.

If you have read Psalm 23:1-4 every day, you will know it very well by now. Use the words as a prayer today.

Don't forget to read the other books.

KING STREET
KING STREET
KING STREET
KING STREET
KING STREET

JESUS THE HELPER

GOD'S SON JESUS
available March 1991

GOD IS GREAT
available March 1991

OUR FATHER GOD

When you've finished the **King Street** series, meet Polly Puter and Sam Sharp in the **'Find Out'** books. They will help you find out more about God as you read your Bible.

There are six **'Find Out'** books to read.

FIND OUT
FIND OUT
FIND OUT

Find Out about Jesus
Find Out about Christians
Find Out about God
Find Out about God's Friends
Find Out about Bible People
Find Out about God's World

Ask your local Christian bookshop or national **Scripture Union** office for more details.

Scripture Union